fairy
houses

of the maine coast

by maureen heffernan

photos by robert mitchell
unless otherwise noted

Down East

Copyright © 2010 by Maureen Heffernan
Photographs by Robert Mitchell except:
Ben Magro - pgs. 12, 18, 28, 54.
Chad Hughes - pgs: 34, 44(top right), 45(top left).
Bill Cullina - pgs: 26, 52(top and bottom left), 64.
Barbara Freeman - pgs. 20,22 (top right), 56 (bottom left), 62.
Maureen Heffernan - pg 68

ISBN: 978-0-89272-787-2

Library of Congress Cataloging-in-Publication Data available on request

Printed in China

5 4 3 2 1

BOOKS·MAGAZINE·ONLINE
www.downeast.com

Distributed to the trade by National Book Network

Designed by Lynda Chilton

Cover Photo by Ben Magro.
Fairy House by Sharmon Provan.

Extracts from F*lower Fairies of the Trees and Flower Fairies of the Garden.* Copyright
© The Estate of Cicely Mary Barker, 1940, 1944.
Reproduced by kind permission of Frederick Warne & Co.

To my mother, who made a
fairy cake for my brother and sister
and me one spring morning,
and "who steered the ship,"
and to my father, who told us
Irish fairy stories and loved
the outdoors.

Contents

Foreword

Those of us who were fortunate enough to spend many childhood days out of doors, and immersed in nature, often have a sense of another, unseen world intersecting with our own, because we directly experienced how nature itself is so endlessly magical and full of wonder.

For me, the portal to that magical world was a small woodland behind our barn, an abandoned nursery site where the ground was hummocky and filled with nooks and holes. My siblings and I called this area "Fairyland" because of those mysterious craters. Encouraged by our parents, we wholeheartedly believed the holes had been made by fairies. We played there for hours, often placing branches over the hollows to create secret dens where we would hide, becoming like fairies and wood sprites ourselves. Even today, that little forest patch holds great enchantment for me.

One early spring morning when I was about six years old, my brother and sister and I got up as usual on a Saturday morning and, after breakfast, my mother told us

excitedly to go out and look for something she spotted near Fairyland. We ran outside to see what it could be and spotted what looked like a large chocolate cake. Decorated with twigs and pebbles, we couldn't believe our eyes. Where did this come from? Who could have made it and left it here? Our mother and father had joined us and they said, it looks like the fairies made it. We were thrilled. This proved that fairies lived in our Fairyland. We thought it must have been a big birthday cake for a fairy or a cake to celebrate spring since the grass was greening up and daffodils and forsythia were blooming in our farmyard.

We were blessed to have a mother and father who knew the importance of creating wonderful childhood memories. Of course, it was my mother who got up early that day and made a big mudcake for us to discover.

My childhood experiences in woods and gardens influenced me to go into a career in horticulture, where I have been fortunate to be able to create new gardens where people (and perhaps even fairies!) can experience the magic, wonder, joy, and solace of nature.

Like Celtic lands, where fairy lore comes from, Maine seems to me to be one of the world's great fairy haunts.

When I moved here and discovered the local tradition of building fairy houses, I was charmed by these delightful little abodes in the woods—each one so unique and almost heartbreakingly sweet and sincere.

I hope this book captures the spirit of place and charm of these fairy houses—both the ones built by children of all ages and the ones found in nature that provide the sweet little hiding places for our fairy friends. ❧

The Road to Fairyland

Do you seek the road to Fairyland?
    I'll tell; it's easy, quite.
Wait till a yellow moon gets up o'er purple
    seas by night,
And gilds a shining pathway that is sparkling
    diamond bright
Then, if no evil power be nigh to thwart you,
    out of spite,
And if you know the very words to cast a spell
    of might,
You get upon a thistledown, and if the breeze
    is right,
You sail away to Fairyland
Along this track of light.
    —Ernest Thompson Seton

A Sense of Fairies

Fairyland

A fairy's house stands in a wood,
Midst fairy trees and flowers,
Where daisies sing like little birds
Between the sun and showers,
And grasses whisper tiny things
About this world of ours.

Some day shall we two try to find
This enchanted place?
Go hand in hand through flower-lit woods
Where living trees embrace
And suddenly, as in a dream,
Behold a fairy's face!

—Maud Keary

The term *faerie* or *fairy* comes from the Latin term *fata,* meaning "fate." Fairies are a "host of super-natural beings and spirits who occupy a limbo between earth and heaven."

—*The Encyclopedia of Witches and Witchcraft*

As children we seem to readily believe in fairies, and even as care-worn adults part of us still enjoys imagining that maybe, just maybe, the woods and fields may harbor these earth spirits.

Woods and meadows are so alive, teeming with scampering, jumping, flying creatures, that because they mostly shy away or hide when a human approaches, it almost seems like there is a real but secret world separate from our own out in the woods and meadows. The concept of fairies must have sprung from the experience of sensing all these little beings who dance and flutter and dart just past our range of vision. Fairies seem to be the folktale embodiment of all the buzzing, fluttering, winging goings-on in nature.

It is easy to sense this unseen world when the darkness changes our perceptions and leaves us feeling more vulnerable. Out in the woods at night, an old tree stump can look like a crouching bear and flying bats can feel like the Furies descending on us from a bad dream. Our sense of hearing becomes more acute than our sight—we hear animal calls, rustling, and other sounds made by unseen creatures. This may be why fairies are said to be especially active at night.

It seems a powerful and persistent ancestral memory —this feeling that, as we walk in the woods and meadows, myriad little beings are hiding in their lairs, nests, and burrows, watching us as we pass by. Why else would fairy stories and folklore be common to all continents and people?

Fairies explain so much that we don't see happening. How do the flowers get their colors? Why, fairies paint them! Fairies also seem to be a manifestation of our longing for a carefree life, a joyful and simple existence of merriment, benign mischief, and play. ❧

Victorian Fairies

Different eras depict fairies differently. The Victorians, in particular, painted and poeticized about them in sweet, cozy, playful, and whimsical ways, as in this verse by an unknown author.

The woods are full of fairies!
The trees are all alive;
The river overflows with them,
See how they dip and dive!
What funny little fellows!
What dainty little dears!
They dance and leap, and prance and peep,
And utter fairy cheers!

"It's easy to believe in magic when you're young. Anything you couldn't explain was magic then. It didn't matter if it was science or a fairy tale. Electricity and elves were both infinitely mysterious and equally possible—elves probably more so."

—Charles de Lint

Fairy Lore

While every part of the world seems to have stories about magical and whimsical creatures, in the west, fairy stories seem most associated with Ireland, Britain, and Germany.

The fairies of western European folklore are tiny, very clever, magical winged creatures, yet also like humans in many ways. They are among the many "earth spirit" creatures said to live deep in the woods, underground, in fields, and along streams and rivers, including gnomes, leprechauns, pixies, brownies, and elves.

Fairies, like humans, create shelters and gather food for themselves. They fashion their clothing from plants in order to camouflage themselves from us. Fairies are thought to especially love flowers and gardens. But mostly, fairies are known for their love of making merry—singing and dancing by the light of the moon or fairy bonfires. Their dancing space is said to be an enchanted circle bounded by a ring of toadstools, stones, or trees. Tradition holds that humans who happen to stumble into

a fairy ring will have a spell cast over them and remain in an enchanted state until physically pulled from the ring. (Might this folklore have anything to do with imaginative explanations for a late night out?)

Fairies are mostly thought to be good-hearted, but tales of playful mischief abound, too. They are said to be able to change their shapes or become invisible if approached by humans. Tradition holds that to keep fairies from playing tricks on you, you should leave small gifts in the woods for them—such as a fairy cake or a fairy house. 🌀

Opposite top left: Legend has it that to avoid being seen, fairies can turn themselves into toadstools until you pass by them.

Opposite top right: Found in the Maine woods: a fairy ring with arch. Fairies are known to dance at midnight within rings of trees, stones, or toadstools.

Opposite bottom: Viewed with an imaginative eye, these weeping spruce trees appear like robed woodland wizards walking down a hillside at Coastal Maine Botanical Gardens.

If you see a faery ring
In a field of grass,
Very lightly step around,
Tip-toe as you pass,
Last night faeries frolicked there,
And they're sleeping somewhere near.

If you see a tiny fairy,
Lying fast asleep
Shut your eyes
And run away,
Do not stay to peek!
Do not tell
Or you'll break a faery spell.

— William Shakespeare

The Enchantments of Maine

Maine's rocky shores, stony soils, and old fields framed by stone walls are reminiscent of Ireland. And like Ireland, Maine seems to be one of the world's great fairy haunts. Perhaps a few fairies stowed away across the sea to North America and sought out places that reminded them of their Old World homelands. With its lush, stream-rich woods and rocky shores, Maine would have been a perfect new home. Its boreal nature has an otherworldly character, inspiring us to look and listen deeply and sense an unseen realm of earth spirits drawn here by the carpets of moss, the lichen-covered ledges, the sounds of waves and sea birds and splashing waterfalls, the fragrance of pine forests, and the winter skies splattered with twinkling stars. Of course, fairies must be here. How can they resist being here?

This sense of magic in the air perhaps explains why Mainers developed a fairy-house-building tradition. It's a tradition that seems to be growing in popularity today as people of all ages want to connect more with nature and spend more

time outside. Building fairy houses is simple, thoughtful, fun. A way for us to exercise our creativity and bond with nature—all the while using our own imaginations.

Maine islands, in particular, are linked with the tradition of building fairy houses. ***Monhegan Island,*** the best

Visiting Fairy House Villages in Maine

Coastal Maine Botanical Gardens
Open all year. Children and families can build fairy houses in the Fairy Village. CMBG also hosts an annual Fairy House Festival in August. Located on Barters Island Road in Boothbay.
Tel. 207-633-4333
www.mainegardens.org

Mackworth Island
Open to the public year-round and accessible by car. From I-295 in Portland, take Exit 9 North to Route 1 and cross the Martins Point Bridge. Take the third right onto Andrews Road to the causeway (follow signs for Baxter School for the Deaf). Stop at the guard house and turn right to the parking area.

Monhegan Island
Monhegan makes a great day or overnight trip. In summer it is accessible by daily ferries from Port Clyde and Boothbay Harbor:

☙ **Monhegan Boat Line**
(Port Clyde)
207-372-8848
www.monheganboat.com

☙ **Balmy Day Cruises**
(Boothbay Harbor)
207-633-2284 or 800-289-2284
www.balmydayscruises.com

known, is one of Maine's and the world's great magical places. Twelve miles off the mainland and a world away from the everyday, Monhegan is a captivating place of breathtaking beauty. Its beautiful coastline and woods are so enchanting and gorgeous that you are amazed that such a place still exists. This fishing community and artists' enclave is the Maine coast at its finest.

The magic of Monhegan seems to inspire us to acknowledge the fairy realm by building little houses. In the island's Cathedral Woods, tall spruces stand like the pillars of a grand cathedral, drawing our eyes upward. For a generation, this moss-floored forest has been the site of Maine's most well-known and beloved fairy house village. **Note:** Due to too many people building fairy houses there in recent years and damaging plants and mosses in the process, visitors are now asked not to build any new houses. Just enjoy seeing any that you may spot on this enchanted island.

At privately owned *Squirrel Island,* off Boothbay Harbor, fairy houses are also a cherished tradition. Flanking a narrow woodland path is a whole little fairy village. Many of these homes are no ordinary twig domiciles. One

fairy house might boast a "china cabinet" filled with tiny shell dishes, while another features a little garden with "topiary" trees.

Mackworth Island lies just outside of Portland but feels like it's miles away from the city. The small island is circled by a lovely coastal walking trail. About halfway around the circuit is a charming woodland fairy house village with views out to Casco Bay. Some of the houses are built against trees and stumps, while others are freestanding upon the thick, soft cushion of pine needles that cover the forest floor.

Coastal Maine Botanical Gardens, on the mainland in Boothbay, is home to a large fairy house village where all young visitors are encouraged to build their own fairy shelters. Reached by a winding shoreland trail, Fairy Village is enclosed by a twig fence. The seemingly hundreds of fairy shelters inside range from basic lean-tos to fortresses to multilevel homes with gardens and shell swimming pools. Some domiciles, made of larger branches, look like they were made for fairies' bigger gnome relations. During the summer, when hundreds of children build fairy homes there, a vast "fairy sprawl" develops,

Like us, fairies often like to
live near water, and shoreside
treasures such as sea glass
and shells add a beautiful
touch to their dwellings.

with even more wee homes springing up like mushrooms and wildflowers outside the fairy village fence.

Of course, most fairy houses are built in countless backyards and woodlots where children gather sticks, twigs, leaves, moss, pine cones, nuts, stones, bark, shells, flowers, and more to construct little dwellings for the fairies. In doing so, they are also encouraging their imagination, empathy, and creativity to take root and grow. And there is nothing to buy—all this creative play is absolutely free, as the best things usually are.

Make sure you look carefully for all the signs of fairies the next time you are in a Maine garden or walking in the woods. Don't forget to look for nature's fairy houses, too! ✷

Nature's Fairy Houses

Just like children, nature provides cozy nooks, crevices, and tussocks where fairies can hide. Look carefully as you explore outdoors—one of these tiny natural shelters can be the perfect starting point for building your fairy house.

Soft moss a downy pillow makes, and green leaves spread a tent,
Where Faerie fold may rest and sleep until their night is spent.
The bluebird sings a lullaby, the firefly gives a light, The twinkling stars
are candles bright. Sleep, Faeries all, Good Night.

—From "A Faery Song," by Elizabeth T. Dillingham

Look Up!

Look up, look up, at any tree!
There is so much for eyes to see:
Twigs, catkins, blossoms; and blue
Of sky, most lovely, peeping through
Between the leaves, some large, some small,
Some green, some gold before their fall;
Fruits you can pick; fruits out of reach;
And little birds with twittering speech;
And, if you're quick enough, maybe
A laughing fairy in the tree!

—From *Flower Fairies of the Trees,*
by Cicely Mary Barker

A Walk in the Woods

A lady with whom I was riding in the
forest said to me that woods always
seemed to her to wait, as if the genii
who inhabit them suspend their deeds
until the wayfarer had passed onward; a
thought which poetry has celebrated in
the dance of the fairies, which breaks off
on the approach of human feet.
                    —Ralph Waldo Emerson

Quietly walk along a forest path early in the morning
or when the shadows start to fall. Look up in the
treetops or down at the forest floor for fairies. As you
walk, birds may suddenly chirp and sing to warn fairies
of your coming. The scampering in the leaves as something darts away may be a squirrel or skunk, but it could
also be the sound of fairies scurrying to hide.

The woods and medows and shoreline of Maine are filled with fairies. They love the tall pines and the soft fragrant-needled floor beneath. They love the sound of water and of birds, the enveloping fogs, the nooks and crannies that make cozy homes, and the soft mosses that make restful beds. Best of all, they love the homes that children build for them.

Let's explore in the woods and look for fairy houses, small and large, simple and not so simple. ✤

Opposite, top left: It takes a sharp eye to spot this tiniest of fairy shelters perched on a bracket fungus.
Opposite right: Mushrooms make convenient sitting spots near the doorway of a stump fairy house.

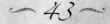

Invite Fairies into Your Garden

Garden fairies come at dawn,
Bless the flowers then they're gone
—Author Unknown

airies celebrate all of nature's enchantments and ephemeral charms before they pass—a full moon, a blooming rose, a rainbow, the morning dew. They love beautiful gardens because they are drawn to the beauty and sweetness of flowers. Legend has it fairies protect gardens and their gardeners if the gardener leaves them little gifts. Invite them into your garden with flowers, trees, and a fairy home built of sticks, stones, and leaves, and a heart that is thankful for nature's everyday miracles.

If you sit ever so quietly in a garden in the early morning, you just might see fairies hovering over hyacinths or roses to breathe in their fragrance or sitting on a water lily leaf dangling their feet in the water. Look for bees and butterflies because fairies love to fly among

You may see fairies cooling off under garden waterfalls . . . or peeping out from inside a tree . . . or swinging from a branch.

Let flower petals drop freely in your garden. It's said that fairies make their clothes from fallen flower petals and sew them together with cobwebs.

them. You might glimpse fairies riding on the backs of the fireflies that flutter through your garden on warm nights. The swishing of tall grasses or rustle of cattails may not be just from the wind; it could be the sound of fairies flitting among the stems. Since fairies can change their shapes, a field full of grasshoppers might also be a field full of fairies jumping about, safe in their shape-shifting disguise. ❧

WHERE

Where are the fairies?
Where can we find them?
We've seen the fairy-rings
They leave behind them!

When they have danced all night,
Where do they go?
Lark, in the sky above,
Say, do you know?
Is it a secret

No one is telling?
Why, in your garden
Surely they're dwelling!

No need for journeying,
Seeking afar:
Where there are flowers,
There fairies are!

—From *Flower Fairies of the Garden,*
by Cicely Mary Barker

Fairies Like Cake, Too!

One morning when I was about six, my mother told my brother and sister and me she had noticed something new out near our Fairyland woods. Of course, we raced out to see what it was—and there, lying at the bottom of a grassy small hill we found what looked like a large chocolate cake. Little twigs were stuck in the cake like birthday candles and small pebbles lined the edge.

Where did this come from? We called for our parents to come take a look. As we all stood around the cake—whose icing now looked a lot like mud, but still delicious—my dad smiled and thoughtfully said, "Well, kids, it looks like the fairies made it. I do believe it's a fairy cake."

Make a Fairy Cake

✔ In the evening, just before it gets dark and the fairies come out to dance and feast, grab a bucket, trowel, and an old milk jug filled with water and head outside.

✔ Mix some garden soil (or you can use potting soil) with a little water to make a thick consistency that holds together when you squeeze a handful of it. Once you have the proportions worked out, make a bigger ball of the mixture and shape it into a large cake or a number of smaller cupcakes. (You can also use a cake mold.)

✔ Decorate your cake with pebbles, twigs, and flower petals, and leave it outside for the fairies!

✔ In winter, fairies love snow cakes decorated with red holly berries and bits of icicles stuck in like candles. In fall, they love red leaves, rose hips, and seeds. Decorate a springtime fairy cake with forsythia and fiddlehead ferns, and in summer use berries and flowers.

✔ If the fairies like your cake, expect them to bring you good luck!

Build Your Own Fairy Houses

rom primitive caves to multi-story edifices, fairy houses can come in all shapes, sizes, and styles limited only by your creativity. Remember, most of all fairies like their houses to be made with things found in nature.

Do be mindful about collecting your natural building materials, however. Be careful not to strip live moss and lichens from trees or rocks, and do not remove bark or cut branches and twigs from living trees or shrubs. Gather fallen branches and twigs and find bark that has been shed naturally, such as the papery curls that drop from birches.

Look for natural nooks and crannies as the starting places for your fairy houses: cavities at the bases of trees, crevices in rock ledges, nooks between moss-covered stones, a hollow stump, the space beneath a fallen log, a natural nest area beneath an arching swath of grass.

If you've chosen a stump or a hollow, or anything with a natural structure already, just begin to decorate. Cover

with moss, add a small door made from a mussel shell for example, or a tree made from a stick with a clump of moss on top. Make tiny stairs of wood bark and windows of sea glass and maybe a miniature rock garden.

If you've found the perfect spot and are going to build a house from scratch, just build a simple structure with sticks bound together or just leaning in to make a tiny teepee, and then cover them with moss, leaves, pine needles, or flowers. Just remember three things.

1. Fairies love privacy and natural beauty.

2. Respect the environment.

3. Have fun.

Once you have completed your first fairy house, you will almost certainly want to build more. You'll start keeping an eye out for ever more types of building materials. Your own "gnome depot" can be that spot in the woods

Gnome Depot is the name for CMBG's Fairy Village building supplies area, *opposite left top.* A massive stone table holds building supplies for Coastal Maine Botanical Gardens' Fairy Village, *opposite middle, left.*

where you find most of your fairy house materials. It can also be the place where you stockpile your special fairy house supplies until you are ready to use them.

Here are some of the building materials you might stock in your own gnome depot:

From woods and meadows:

sticks, twigs, and driftwood

grass

feathers

stones and pebbles

pine, fir, and spruce cones

moss and lichens that have naturally detached
from rocks or tree trunks

bark that has naturally peeled off trees

pine needles, fern fronds

flowers and flower petals

leaves, particularly in autumn

milkweed silk (for beds and pillows) and pods

acorns and acorn caps, beechnuts, and hazelnuts

seeds, berries, and mushrooms

From the shore:

seaweed that has washed up on shore

sea shells: clam, mussel, lobster, whelk, and others

sea glass, smooth stones, pebbles, and sand

From your kitchen and garden:

corn silk

flowers and flower petals

berries

empty walnut shells

sunflower and pumpkin seeds

cocoa shell mulch (fairies and children love
the chocolate smell)

❧

Adhesives

If you become inspired and want to create a more elaborate fairy house, use a hot glue gun or a super glue-type adhesive to fabricate bark walls, attach sticks, and especially to attach moss, acorns, feathers, and other adornments to the structure. Other ways to attach pieces together are to use fine gauge wire, string, or twine, by cutting off some longer roots of uprooted trees you might find in the woods and using them like twine.

No child but must remember laying his head in the grass, staring into the infinitesimal forest and seeing it grow populous with fairy armies.

—From *Essays in the Art of Writing* by Robert Louis Stevenson

No Child Left Indoors

If I had influence with the good fairy who is supposed to preside over the christening of all children, I should ask that her gift to each child in the world be a sense of wonder so indestructible that it would last throughout life. . . .If a child is to keep alive his inborn sense of wonder without any such gift from the fairies, he needs the companionship of at least one adult who can share it, rediscovering with him the joy, excitement and mystery of the world we live in.

—From *The Sense of Wonder*
by Rachel Carson

This is the rallying cry for our times. Children who spend time outside develop a lifelong bond with nature and a curiosity about the natural world that will stay with them their whole lives.

We all need the chance to use our imaginations, to build things out of natural materials, to lose ourselves

with complete focus on a project or imaginative game: building tree houses, making secret woodland forts, damming the little streams that appear after a heavy rain, or planting and tending a small garden.

Creating little fairy houses stimulates collaboration and cooperation. Ideas spill back and forth, creativity is playfully competitive, and before long a new fairy encampment or village appears, with each home uniquely charming—no cookie-cutter subdivision here.

When we build fairy houses we are not only getting nourishment from being outdoors, but we are also thinking creatively and looking at nature's taken-for-granted "raw materials" in a new way. How can I make this side of the house stand up? What can I use to make a roof? Could this piece of curled birch bark make a skateboard ramp for fairy children? And perhaps we just might realize we can have fun without buying anything or turning on a switch or depending on anyone else to entertain us. We can have *more* fun entertaining ourselves in the best playground to be had—in nature. ❧

"Come Fairies, take me out of this dull world, for I would ride with you upon the wind and dance upon the mountains like a flame!"

—William Butler Yeats

Fairy Festivals and Events

Coastal Maine Botanical Gardens' Fairy House Festival
Barters Island Road, Boothbay, ME 04537
207-633-4333

For three days each August, fairies and fairy houses are celebrated and all manner of fairy events take place in gardens and woodlands. Children and families can participate in fairy dances, fairy crafts, fairy storytelling, fairy games, fairy music, fairy teas, and a fairy parade. And, of course, everyone can make a fairy house. The festival is held the second weekend in August. Free with Gardens admission. Visit the Web Site for directions and visitor information: www.mainegardens.org.

Strawbery Banke Museum
14 Hancock Street, Portsmouth, NH 03801
603-433-1100

Strawbery Banke is a museum village of historic homes, gardens, and shops. In mid-September, it offers an annual Fairy House Tour, a self-guided walking tour of fairy houses at its site and throughout the Portsmouth area built by families, garden clubs, artists, and others. Strawberry Banke also has fairy houses on display throughout the summer and fall months in its Victorian Children's Garden. Many of these "better little homes and gardens" will delight you with their craftsmanship and detail. For visiting information, visit www.strawberybanke.org.

**Enchanted Woods™ at Winterthur Museum
& Country Estate**

5105 Kennett Pike, Winterthur, DE 19735
Tel. 800-448-3883

At this former DuPont family estate, now a museum and garden, is a three-acre children's garden called Enchanted Woods™ that is devoted to the folklore of fairies and earth spirits. Set in an oak woods, this garden includes a Faerie Cottage, Tulip Tree House, Fairy Mushroom Ring, a Fairy Flower Labyrinth, an Acorn Tearoom, a Troll Bridge, and a Green Man's Lair. Utterly enchanting, this garden is a must see for fairy and garden lovers of all ages. For information, visit www.winterthur.org.

Acknowledgments

Special thanks to Robert Mitchell who was so terrific to work with and whose artistic eye and photographic skill produced such beautiful and charming images. He always responded when there was a "fairy" moment to capture and he captured them all so superbly.

Thanks also to Barbara Freeman and William Cullina for the use of their creative and expert fairy house and garden photographs.

Monhegan Island

This Maine island is rich in fairy houses, stunning beauty, and magic, and is a place that greatly inspired this book.

Coastal Maine Botanical Gardens

Much of the photography for this book was taken over several years at Coastal Maine Botanical Gardens in its ornamental gardens, natural woodland and shoreland areas, and Fairy Village area.

Sincere thanks and a salute to everyone at Coastal Maine Botanical Gardens who make the garden and fairy magic happen there every day. A heartfelt thanks to all of the staff and volunteers who maintain Maine's most enchanting public fairy house village, gardens, and trails, and produce the gardens' annual fairy house festival.

And, of course, thanks and appreciation to children of all ages who build and leave their little fairy houses all over Maine delighting not only the fairies but anyone who happens to spot one. ❧

Fairy Houses built by:

Amy Collins - pg. 4
David Lee - pg. 8
Steven Wigdzinski - pg. 28
Don Viens - pg 32
Sharmon Provan – pg. 26, 44
Shell house: St. Andrew's Village,
  Boothbay - pgs. 44-45

Andy Abello and Amanda Russell -
High-rise log house - pg. 54/ Winter
Fairy House with chimney
  smoke - pg. 56
Arch and larger fairy houses:
  Cathy Court and David Lee - pg. 56

Sculpture Credit:
The sculpture of the bear in polychromed clay, on page 66, is by Maine artists Squidge Liljeblad, and is part of the permanent sculpture collection at Coastal Maine Botanical Gardens.